In a
ten ...
sler offer a hopeful and practical methodology,
developing deep, shared understandings between
people. Importantly, their methodology embraces
the fact that a pluralistic world thrives on differing views and posits that the goal is not to resolve
differences, but to find connections among those
differences. Uelmen and Kessler potently use their
own teaching experiences and the words of their
students to guide us in how to transform anxiet-
ies about how we are perceived by, and relate to,
others into a steadfastness about the positive pos-
sibilities of engaging. While Uelmen and Kessler
speak most directly to those working with millennials, their advice and five-step methodology can
be embraced by all of us.

Deborah J. Cantrell

Associate Professor & Director,
Clinical Education Program
University of Colorado Law School

Five Steps To Healing Polarization in the Classroom

About the
5 Steps Series

The books in the 5 Steps Series are useful for any-one seeking bridge-building solutions to cur-rent issues. The 5 Steps series presents positive approaches for engaging with the problems that open up gaps and divisions in family, school, church, and society. Each volume presents five short chapters (or "steps") on a single topic. Each chapter includes a relevant "excerpt", "insights" from the author(s), and an "example" to consider. The "example" is a real-life story that illustrates how each step can be applied in daily life.

Five Steps To Healing Polarization in the Classroom

Insights and Examples

Amy Uelmen

Michael Kessler

New City Press
Hyde Park, New York

Published in the United States by New City Press
202 Comforter Blvd.,
Hyde Park, NY 12538
www.newcitypress.com
©2018 Amelia Uelmen/Michael Kessler

Cover design by Leandro de Leon

Library of Congress Control Number: 2017963159
5 steps to healing polarization in the classroom / by Amy
Uelmen and Michael Kessler.

ISBN 978-1-56548-629-4 (paper)
ISBN 978-1-56548-630-0 (e-book)

Printed in the United States of America

Contents

Step 4

Step 5

Introduction

A relational response to polarization

Recent studies indicate a dramatic increase in the partisan divide on political values.[1] It is not a stretch to conclude that faculty and students alike are bringing these divisions into the college and graduate school classroom.[2] Some pedagogical responses to these tensions focus on creating "safe space" for students whose perspectives have been marginalized or silenced due to the subtle or not-so-subtle dynamics of privilege and power. Other educators have critiqued these efforts. We believe that teachers at all levels of education have much to learn by reflecting on these debates, both to gain awareness of their own areas of implicit or explicit bias, and to develop increasingly fine-tuned sensitivities to the challenges that their students from varying backgrounds may face.

However, these questions are not the focus of this book. Instead, we begin with a question: why are millennials—students born in the early 1980s to about 2000—generally reluctant or fearful to discuss their deep differences in a classroom setting? We posit that the key to healing polarization in today's classroom lies in recognizing what lies at the root of this fear: this generation's heightened sensitivity to relationships with their peers. When our pedagogical practices address the frailties and build on the strengths of this heightened sensitivity, this can help to moderate these tensions, and in turn help to heal polarization in a classroom.

The characteristics of the millennial generation have been the subject of much reflection and commentary. Research indicates their focus on care and concern for others. For example, when asked to identify "one of the most important things in their lives," 52% responded being a good parent; 30%, having a successful marriage; 21%, helping others in need; and only 15%, having a high paying career.[3] On the flip side, frailties emerge when this sensitivity takes the form of excessive attention to social appearances. Millennials may also fear that others' preconceptions or judgments may isolate them from their peers. The tension between concern and insecurity can make it difficult to foster robust conversation across profound difference in a variety of social, cultural and educational environments.

How might teachers in a variety of settings help students to acknowledge the source of such tension and use the energy of that realization to amplify the strengths that their heightened sensitivity to relationships may offer? This book details methods that have emerged from team-teaching a graduate level seminar, *Religion, Morality & Contested Claims for Justice.*[4] After a brief explanation of our foundations, we outline five steps to help students move toward a more thoughtful reflection process that helps them to develop communication skills so as to foster attentive respect and openness to other students' ideas and identities.

Our method is based on a few basic principles. First, our class engages issues that touch upon the deepest levels of personal and communal identity. The readings and our discussions probe deeply-held assumptions, ethical aspirations, and moral norms underlying contested policy and legal issues. We invite this inquiry with the conviction that a pedagogical space should allow students to explore the values and norms often overlooked in the policy-making discussions. This helps uncover the many meanings and tensions operating within policy debates and also brings to the surface unperceived disagreements and differences over underlying premises and principles.

Second, we believe that our primary role as teachers is to help students explore their own and others' views and by reflection to tease out the underlying connections and tensions between their views and those of others in the wider horizon of the conversations. As they approach these issues from many angles, our students manifest divergent, even irreconcilable, positions. Some have thought long and hard about what supports their policy positions; some very little. They comprise a spectrum of opinions—progressives, conservatives, deeply pious, agnostic, radicals, skeptical, and indifferent. Each student has wrestled with their upbringing and the historical, cultural, and moral influences that have shaped their views; few have entirely consistent positions across policy issues and moral norms.

Third, our goal is not to change our students' minds about their substantive positions. Rather, we seek to complicate and develop their own reflection about the issues and give respectful, patient reflection upon others' positions and views. We model for students, and encourage them to adopt what we call "a hermeneutics of goodwill." This involves seeking a fair and comprehensive interpretation and analysis of an author's or classmate's position before rushing to judge critically or dismiss the position. This hermeneutic also involves resisting the urge to impose a framework on a position because of readily-available proxies (e.g. "this is a liberal/conservative argument that I need not take seriously since I disagree with the outcome/conclusion"). Part of developing a critical and reflective appreciation for arguments over policy in light of the underlying norms and values expressed in those policies is allowing the complexity of the positions to come into the foreground.

Finally, our method is intended to address policy positions not as isolated kernels of thought floating in the ideological ether but as positions that people have adopted and applied in real lives. A hermeneutic of goodwill requires a more comprehensive engagement with the full scope of the arguments around a policy position, its underlying premises, *and* the narrative histories and identities of those who advance the arguments. The chains of reasoning people use to draw a conclusion about a policy issue are unique to them, involving reflection (of varying degrees of sophistication), intuition, emotion, and varying degrees of acceptance or rejection of their own history, culture, and experiences. We advocate neither deference nor acquiescence. Approaching a person with whom you disagree, while seeking to recognize and understand the full complexity of how they have arrived at their position, requires solicitude and patience, even while the goal may be to discern critically where you disagree and fully articulate a judgment of the deficiencies of others' positions.

We engage this method where disagreements over reasonably held positions may arise. We acknowledge that situations might arise where a speaker advocates for certain kinds of violence or for excluding certain persons from social discourse on the basis of their gender, race, creed, or ethnicity, among other factors. For instance, we admit reasonable disagreement and open conversation about conscientious accommodations in the realm of same-sex marriage but disallow statements that degrade or dehumanize persons who are homosexual. Societal norms and local customs will also inform what is out of bounds in a particular classroom. Our method does not specify how to set those boundaries. We have generally been fortunate that our students have not advocated positions hostile to other students' safety and well-being. Nevertheless, some readers may face the real possibility of having to affirm a boundary and rebut or disallow statements that deny the basic dignity of others. It is a challenge, however, to set boundaries for effective dialogue concerning divisive issues without exacerbating the polarization.

Five Steps to Healing Polarization in the Classroom

An initial word on the "mechanics" of our pedagogical method for a discussion-based seminar. We ask students to turn in reflection papers twenty-four hours in advance of the seminar meeting time. Based on these, we formulate an agenda that is circulated prior to the class discussion, helping students come into the class meeting with the perception of a potential conversational connection with their peers. In our experience, when students are encouraged to refine habits of reflection and are aided in perceiving potential conversational connections, the organic result frequently is the formation of a community that stretches across multiple political, ethnic, social and religious differences. In this context they can work to hone the communication and dialogue skills that will help them to respect, engage, and learn from others who think differently. This context also offers an opportunity to reflect on how their own rhetorical choices may be received and understood by people with whom they may differ in some respect.

The five steps presented in this book aim to help each student in the class to:

1. Prioritize reflective over reactive habits of mind

2. Discern the potential for conversational connections with other colleagues

3. Be fully present and engaged in the classroom discussion

4. Actively take responsibility for full participation by all members of the class

5. Learn to lean into disagreement and conflict

The sections that follow describe in more detail each pedagogical step. Our own students provide examples of how these methods have informed their thought process, growth and engagement with others who think differently.

We have worked out these methods in the context of relatively small (15-20 students) discussion-based seminars that focus on how personal and religious values intersect with questions of law, politics and public policy. We realize that larger settings and time constraints limit the practicality of implementing some of our suggestions. For this reason, the book concludes with a reflection on how the methods may be adapted for diverse educational settings.

Step *1*

Prioritize Reflective Over Reactive Habits of Mind

ON THE SEMINARS THAT WE teach, assigned reading is intended first of all as a springboard for weekly written reflections. Readings from a range of political, religious, and social perspectives invite students to encounter differing intellectual positions and cultural views on contested topics. We also invite students to suggest which texts to remove, or which to add. Course topics are paced so that the most polarizing questions are addressed after the class has developed an increased level of trust.

We recognize that students are busy, often juggling the demands of several classes and other activities, as well as work and family responsibilities. For this reason, we allow students to alternate between submitting shorter "blurbs" and longer four-page reflection papers. Within a given block of two classes, students may choose which week to write the longer submission. In our experience, if the due dates for longer reflections are not carefully structured, many students leave the papers for the end of the semester, at times delaying deeper engagement. Papers are due twenty-four hours in advance, to facilitate formulating a shared agenda, described below. So students can focus on the reflection papers throughout the semester, our seminars do not include a comprehensive final exam.

In a law school seminar setting this is unusual (most seminars require only a final paper), but students have affirmed that it is an intellectually enriching process. "I realized that I don't even know what I think," is a surprisingly common response to taking an extended period to reflect on controversial questions. Because they are immersed in contrastive opinions about cultural or political questions, often stated forcefully, by reflection students learn how these strong undercurrents pull them in one direction or another. For many, developing a habit of weekly reflection that culminates in a written result begins a process of de-toxification from such "reactive" habits of mind.

At the same time, we also emphasize that submissions should not become mere diaries or journal entries. Although the students' submissions may provide the space to explore the intersection between personal values and public arguments, and we encourage attention to the emotional dimension of the topics we address, we expect their work to provide a springboard for public discussion. We also emphasize analytic precision, organization, and other criteria that will help them to hone their invaluable professional skill in "writing short." Writing projects that bring together personal and professional dimensions help many students learn to pose questions that require a deeper sense of integration.

We realize that current classroom technology facilitates the exchange of written submissions, among even large numbers of students. Notwithstanding the ease of sharing electronic documents among all students in class, we generally ask students to submit their papers only to us as professors. We believe this submission process prioritizes reflection in several ways.

First, students of this generation feel a pervasive sense of always being "on," as if performing before a camera. They experience this in their social expectations, motivation to succeed and even in postings on social media. Constant interaction with these forums makes finding their own reflective voice more difficult. Especially at the beginning of the semester, focusing on having them critique other students' writing style or analytic approach could prevent them from scrutinizing how they themselves think and how they express their thoughts. For this reason, we do not offer "model" or "sample" essays that exhibit an "ideal" approach to the assignment when students ask for them. Furthermore, in light of their fears about appearing judgmental, especially when discussions focus on difficult issues such as abortion, death, or sexual identity, maintaining a zone of privacy allows students to express themselves without worrying about how their analysis could be perceived as a judgment of others.

A second reason for initial submission only to the professor is that students may feel isolated if they post a reflection to a large group, but cannot tell if anyone is paying attention. Most students are too busy to dedicate time to thoughtful appreciation of each other's work. As described below, when we do ask them to read each other's work in preparation for small group discussions, we ask them to focus on a manageable number (two or three) of their colleagues' papers and reduce the size of the reading assignment. Generally, we schedule such exercises later in the semester, after students have developed their writing style and a level of trust has been built among the seminar participants.

A third reason for having students submit papers only to the professor is to facilitate the reflective process for students with unpopular views or minority positions. Students with such opinions otherwise might hold back from class discussion or blunt the argument they might want to present. Submission only to the professor provides a buffer against the peer pressure and doctrinal normativity that pervades some modern university classrooms. A modicum of privacy can help to provide the intellectual space students need to develop their argument and prepare it for public discussion.

Finally, many issues that we broach in our seminars may touch deeply personal dimensions. Submission just to the professor leaves a "release valve" whereby pain or anger can emerge in a way that respects the student's privacy and avoids, as much as possible, "oversharing." Especially when students have experienced a particular trauma, it can be helpful to reflect in writing before entering into public discussion. Further, knowing that a supportive professor is listening to them and guarding their privacy helps students discern how to voice even painful topics in a public conversation.

What happens when every student in a discussion-based class prepares a written reflection prior to the discussion? Such writing generates an investment in the class, as evidenced in high attendance and active participation. Prior reflection and writing helps students who struggle to bring their voice to seminar discussions by increasing their confidence and helping them recollect their thoughts. For those who are naturally talkative, prior reflection helps them focus and synthesize their ideas. For all students, having one's own written contribution as a foundation for the discussion generates a conversation less bound by fears of what others are thinking, and more open to learning what others have worked out during their own reflection.

In students' words
The value of reflection

"What makes me rigid?" When my classmate first posed this question out loud in class, my first thought was what an obvious question that was. Then I realized that I had never once in my twenty-four years asked myself that question. I mulled it over for a few weeks. What makes me unable to adapt and inflexible when others open up and share their thoughts with me?

I am rigid when I am hypersensitive to people's comments and I automatically assume I know what the other person means by his or her words. There have been countless times in my life when I unconsciously chose to be offended due to something someone—be it a close friend, family members, or acquaintance—said to me, rather than probing for the reason and the meaning beneath the words. In those situations, I become too preoccupied with thinking of myself as a misunderstood victim (for lack of a better word) and miss opportunities to further the existing discourse.

I am also rigid because of personal experiences that have made me fear and altogether avoid discourse on specific topics—most notably my experience as a survivor of rape. It was hurtful to hear classmates in another class argue whether "no" actually means "yes" or whether a rape victim deserves justice because she did not fight against her abuser. My avoidance was—and still is, but hopefully to a lesser extent as I grew more aware of it—a form of protection. Before taking this class, I viewed this avoidance as others silencing me. Others had stolen my voice through their hurtful and insensitive comments.

However, through this class, I have come to the conclusion I silenced myself. This was not an easy conclusion to come to because it meant having to recognize and admit my responsibility in my own predicament. The respect we fostered as a class allowed me to open up in a public setting as I had never done before. I have also deeply appreciated instances in which my classmates put aside their rigidity to answer my questions, however poorly phrased they were, and to share their narratives with me. Their sincerity and the trust we built in the class was a true gift.

Finally, I am rigid because I easily accept whatever I read, see, or hear from the media and within my social environment. Before taking this class, I thought I had formed opinions that I could honestly call my own. Nonetheless, as I sat down once a week to write my reflection paper, I came to the sad realization that I had never questioned my opinions enough to figure out why I held them beyond sweeping generalizations. In class, being confronted with opposing views helped define my own. If I agreed with someone, what was it about their opinion that I aligned myself with? If I disagreed, what specifically did I disagree with and how could I justify my own views? As such, I am at the very least much more aware of my tendency to take in things without questioning them.

Anonymous (included with permission)

Step 2

Discern Potential Conversational Connections With Other Colleagues

OW WE COME TO THE "SEcret sauce" of our pedagogical method. As noted in the introduction, we believe that one of the principal reasons for polarization in the classroom is students feeling isolated because they are fearful of being judged and of being perceived by their peers as judging others. Often, they believe that they are the only person in the room to speak from a certain perspective, to hold a certain belief or to harbor certain doubts or questions. These fears can make them extremely reluctant to move into contested or difficult topics of conversation.

Some work hard to crack the group's own communication code revealed through "virtue signaling"—which indicates the limited number of arguments, and perhaps even phrases, that are morally acceptable in conversation among the group. Some classrooms resemble "echo chambers" where it is difficult to bring nuanced differences in perspectives to the surface. In those classrooms it is difficult for students to observe and model the communication skills required for conversation across significant differences and disagreements.

What pedagogical methods might help to address this concern? At the heart of our method is what we do with the reflection papers and blurbs that students submit twenty-four hours before the class discussion. In formulating an agenda for the class discussion we do not presume to use class time to "cover" the material that we have proposed. At times, the material may have suggested to one or the other of us as professors a particular focus, or even well-developed scholarship. If the students have not picked up on those questions, we work hard to resist the temptation to steer the class meeting to what we find interesting. This is not to say that we never raise themes except those that emerge from the students' essays. We do incorporate our own interests when we see that it may be helpful. But we aim to shape the class agenda around the students' reflections.

Once we have identified themes based on the questions and focal points that emerge from the students' papers, we note each of their names beside one or more areas for discussion,[5] and then circulate the agenda the evening prior to our class meeting. On the surface, an agenda for discussion may seem to be simply an organizational tool to keep a seminar on track. But students realize and accept that often something deeper is taking place.

First, this method signals that the professor is listening with attention to each student, and that each student's contribution is a valuable element of the work that the whole class is doing. An agenda drawn from student reflections also "de-centers" the classroom, away from a linear focus on the professors' personal or professional desires and toward circular acknowledgement of the variety of perspectives in the room. To further emphasize this shift, we also allow students to add to or edit the agenda after they receive it the evening before our class meeting. For example, if any student feels that agenda does not include their position or particular interest we encourage them to critique our draft. By doing this, individually and as a group the students build a sense of trust, personal investment in, and attention to their written submissions. In fact, we have often seen the students' writing improve dramatically over the course of the semester, generated we presume, at least in part, by this increased investment and attention.

Second, an agenda circulated prior to the class functions like a group picture in which they can see themselves and their own ideas in relation to others in the group. It is interesting to note that students of the millennial generation tend to locate themselves not so much according to how they receive shared *answers*, but in their perception of shared *questions*. Many students are surprised and relieved to see their names grouped with others in a way that communicates others too are concerned with certain themes, or are posing certain questions. When they realize that they are not alone, they come into the class with a more confident, open and curious spirit.

Many have shared that they are especially pleased to see their name grouped with someone who they would not have considered a "friend," or who they thought to be on the opposite end of the political spectrum. In other words, an agenda helps them to situate themselves not only in relationship to the material, or to the professor's thought, but in relation to *each other*. This in turn helps to reduce or eliminate the anxiety that one's position might be perceived as judgmental, or that one might be judged by others.

As discussed in Step Four, reflection papers can also serve as an invaluable instrument in organizing small group discussions, whether grouped by themes of common interest or grouped to have participants encounter various kinds of difference (e.g., religious, political, etc.).

In students' words
The value of a pre-circulated agenda

From the students' perspective, a pre-circulated agenda serves two purposes: first, as an aid to further reflection and deliberate recollection of one's thoughts prior to the class discussion; and second, as an opportunity to catch an encouraging glimpse of how one's own ideas "fit" within the larger group.

On the first point, Stephanie N. explains the specific benefits for students who process ideas in a more "introverted" way: "As an introvert, I find the circulation of an agenda prior to class to be very valuable. I dislike being put "on the spot" or surprised by a turn in the discussion. As a result, I tend to spend most of those classes (that do not have pre-circulated agendas) absorbing and reflecting internally, rather than contributing to the class. Of course, by distributing the agenda early, you run the risk of having some students arriving to class with a canned response only to disengage from the discussion afterwards because they have already spoken up. But most of the time I believe the result is the opposite. A pre-circulated agenda allows for a deeper than surface level discussion of the topics at hand. I can come prepared with fully fleshed out ideas or thoughtful questions."

Chris C. highlights similar benefits: "Sometimes we cover difficult and controversial topics in class, and having the agenda is helpful because it allows me some time to sift through some of my own thoughts and prepare to contribute to a certain section of the discussion. It helps facilitate participation by allowing us time to think though how our reflection and participation fits within the class as a whole."

On the second point, Kyle H. found it "extremely handy" to know "going into the class where everyone else had taken the readings. Unlike some more straight-forward classes, the readings in our class could be read from countless perspectives, so entering the class knowing a bit about the different perspectives we were going to be discussing made it much easier to ease into."

Megan R. affirmed: "I felt the agenda was invaluable — it gave me a frame of mind as to what we would be discussing during class, and I knew what to expect. It also allowed me to think ahead of time about differing opinions among the class and how people perceived the readings and the topics. I think it also made me more willing to participate because I felt my comments 'belonged,' if that makes sense — like no one was going to look at me as though I had three heads for what I was thinking, based on seeing how other people framed the issues ahead of time."

Step 3

Be Fully Present and Engaged in the Seminar Discussion

REPARING STUDENTS TO BE fully present and engaged in the classroom discussion includes setting up the classroom space so that each student can see everyone else's face—both the professor's and other students' faces, and as much as possible, to read each other's body language. Especially at the beginning of the course, name placards help to encourage a personal connection among everyone in the class. One of the greatest obstacles to students and professors alike being fully present and engaged, however, is distraction from laptops and cell phones. Suggestions for helping all of us to "unplug" from technology follow.

Unplug from distractions due to technology

Recent research discusses circumstances in which laptops may *not* enhance student learning in the classroom.[6] Here we emphasize how personal interactions with technology can thwart the desired atmosphere especially for a discussion-based class that includes highly-charged topics.

At the beginning of the semester (for this kind of seminar) we used to give an "I hate laptops" speech. Now, instead, we ask the students to list why we might ban laptops; they articulate their own reasons convincingly. One student seemed to speak for everyone: "I am fortunate enough to be in two classes this semester that ban laptops." As noted in the student reflections below, having a seminar space without laptops cultivates habits of mindfulness.

For many, the distraction of using apps and computer programs not related to the class discussion undermines the trust needed to open out difficult and sensitive topics. Why would students risk venturing into potentially fraught territory if their would-be conversation partners are preoccupied with shopping, surfing, emailing or playing games? Even one person in the room engaging in such activities can disrupt the conversation, not only because that person's screen is a distraction to those sitting nearby, but because of its effect on the tone in the classroom—that other students' interventions are not worthy of full attention.

As students learn to appreciate the art and skill of listening, and the hard work this entails, they pay increasing attention to body language—their own, and that of others. A physical screen can interfere with this work.

Some students take notes on their laptops as if taking dictation when their professors speak, but almost ignoring what their fellow students say. These audible rhythms of punctuated attention over-emphasize the professor's authority. Closing the laptops fosters a more "circular" environment and establishes a positive atmosphere in which anyone who speaks gets full attention. Closing the laptops also helps students to be present not only to the others in the class, but also to themselves, and to their own thought process.

Obsessive attention to cell phone messages during class poses similar obstacles. We and our students have noticed that when everyone dives into their cell phones during a break, we miss an opportunity to strengthen the bonds of trust emerging in the class through informal connections and chit-chat. Such spontaneous exchanges lead to deeper friendships and nurture a capacity for human connection.[7] Professors too can model the capacity to unplug, whether during class, breaks, or office hours, and so give students their full attention.

Get everyone to unplug

It is hard to unplug. Doing so can be encouraged by linking detachment from technology with the process of reflection and to professional skills and competency: the ability to distinguish objective emergencies that require immediate attention from distractions that feed unhealthy and reactive habits of mind. For example, students responsible for small children or ill or elderly relatives can develop a system for responding to true emergencies while filtering out other distractions. All students can probably benefit by a break from multi-tasking.

Students who want to refer to their own papers during class can print a paper copy. In our seminars, we distribute copies of the agenda at the beginning of class. Finally, we reassure those students concerned about having a detailed set of notes by explaining the nature of their final project. We do not ask for detailed recall of the content of the material, but engagement with the process of generating thoughtful discussion. The school makes audio and video recordings of class discussions, which we make readily available for students in the seminar. After each class, we also circulate a cell-phone picture of notes on the chalkboard.

In students' words
The value of banning laptops

Most of our students feel strongly that in a small seminar that focuses on questions of identity, laptops are distracting or even destructive. To write their final reflection papers, students need only the Agenda (discussed above) and cell phone pictures of the themes recorded on the chalkboard as they emerge throughout the discussion.

Chris C. explains: "In seminars built upon discussion and participation it's imperative that there are no laptops. I think laptops have value in some [more doctrinal] classes, but in these types of seminars I find them distracting and unnecessary—especially when everything written on the board is photographed and recorded. Without laptops, I'm much more in tune with the flow of the discussion and I'm far more willing to pay attention to other students. I get distracted very easily when I have my laptop out in class, so perhaps I'm a bit biased. Nonetheless, there's nothing worse than sharing something from your soul only to look around the room and see a dozen Apple logos on the back of people's computers."

Stephanie N. agrees: "As much as I hate being without my laptop, I think it's really important to ban laptops from seminars. It creates an environment that is much more conducive to meaningful exchanges. Some professors acknowledge that students sometimes are googling more information to contribute to the class but most of the time students are zoning out, reading the news or scrolling through Facebook. Banning laptops during class discussion also promotes mindfulness. Absence of distractions (texts, emails, notifications, news articles) from your laptop allows students to give speakers and each other their full attention, leading to a more engaged and rewarding class."

Kate T. affirms: "I loved the no laptop rule. I wish every class was a no laptop zone, to be honest. I love being able to unplug!"

Alex E. writes: "I think the 'unplugging' is huge. With a screen in front of me and the web at my fingertips I would have been a lot more likely to escape into my computer to avoid the introspection and vulnerability required in these seminars. And it is not that these classes are so uncomfortable that I was ever consciously looking for an escape, it's just that I know that I reflexively escape like that at the slightest prompting whenever a computer is stationed between me and other people. Maybe more importantly, I feel less silly being vulnerable when I know I am not competing for my classmates' attention with whatever is on their screens."

Megan R. also affirms: "I loved not having our laptops and phones out. While I am sure it mostly had to do with the subject matter and how important it is in my life, I think the no-laptops policy also led to me feeling more engaged and focused than I have in most classes. I also liked the fact that there were no notes to take. The nature of the class put me incredibly at ease because I did not need to be taking notes or remembering tiny details in preparation for an exam. I was being present, and that is something I have been trying to work on in my life."

Kyle H. was "neutral" about banning laptops because of his experience in small class settings where they did not distract from engagement and because he valued being able to refer to readings online. Nonetheless he agreed that the ban "sets a good mood, establishing that the outside world is cut off for a couple hours;" and helps seminar colleagues "look and feel more open and accessible."

Jill M. notices how difficult it is for students to break with the habit of discussing polarizing questions online, where, she writes, people are "largely shielded from the impact of their words and rarely have presumptions challenged from someone they see as fully human. This makes face to face conversations even more challenging, because they have been wired to say exactly what they think, with little regard to how it is received. It is never received by a real person, just a screen name."

Instead, in the Contested Claims seminar, she noticed "many times . . . I heard people talking one on one to clarify possible misunderstandings or to ask follow up questions. It truly became the culture of the class." Jill herself gives an excellent example of the benefits of staying unplugged during a break: "One of my classmates raised a supposedly rhetorical question during the class discussion, one that I felt made some pretty damning presumptions about American women. She was not from the US, so what to her was a simple rhetorical question actually had quite a complex answer. During the break, I approached her and we discussed it. She thanked me for providing important information that helped her understand why a particular issue was a point of controversy in the US. I also realized that had I been operating from the same set of presumptions, I very likely would have held the same views about the law that she did."

Step *4*

Both Professors and Students Promote Full Participation by All Members of the Class

O N DISCUSSION-BASED CLASSES of any size, it is challenging when a few particularly loquacious or extroverted students dominate the oral conversation. As discussed above, written reflection prior to class time is one way to remedy this imbalance. Two further suggestions are discussed below.

Every student speaks every class

When class size and meeting time allows, even participation can be facilitated by establishing this rule: "Every student speaks every class." This rule is most effective if presented to the whole class early in the semester as a goal for each class meeting. If all seminar members own the shared goal of creating an environment where every student feels comfortable speaking, every session can be structured to offer every student an opportunity to speak.

It is generally helpful to let students themselves choose when to intervene in the discussion, as discussed above, but circulating an agenda prior to class can suggest points at which students might offer their contribution. During our weekly two-hour seminars, we take a tally at the break of the voices not yet heard, and when we reconvene we reinforce our shared project of making room for every voice.

Small group discussions to hone the art of listening

Small group discussions based on prior reflection can also foster active participation by cultivating the art of listening. Once the group has reached a certain level of trust, we sometimes invite small group members to read each other's reflection papers as a further entry point into each other's perspectives. On these occasions, we give students a "heads up" so that they can adjust their reflections to a potentially more varied audience. We also reduce the reading load in order to encourage giving careful thought to their colleagues' work.

Because small group discussions are not mediated or moderated by a professor's presence, we also prepare the ground for fruitful discussion, especially regarding areas of potential tension or conflict. We emphasize concrete ways to express in their relationships with each other respect, openness, attention, humility, and gratitude. An example follows:

1. **"Take off your shoes."** Convey that respect for the sacred story, dignity, presence, of another human being is much more important than getting points across. Using an image frequently invoked to convey God's radical otherness—the burning bush—Pope Francis suggests that we "remove our sandals before the sacred ground of the other (cf. *Ex* 3:5)." Reflect on how you might help others understand that you do not intend to stomp on their story, their identity, and especially the areas where they feel vulnerable or fragile. This can go a long way in building the trust needed to hold conversations in areas of disagreement.

2. **Unplug from technology** to convey an attitude and posture of full attention. If possible, also remove temptations to constantly check time. If as a potential emergency or another urgent matter require keeping track of messages, explain the circumstances to your conversation partners. Sit in a way that conveys openness and a readiness to listen, with heart and mind focused. Let others read your facial expressions and body language in order to build mutual understanding.

3. When discussing a text or listening to a perspective that you do not fully understand or with which you may disagree, give yourself and the other person an "out" by **admitting that you may not have full information,** or that you may not have elements that allow you to grasp the ideas. This avoids painting yourself or the other into a corner. Learn to ask sincere questions that leave the other space to frame the new information according to their own criteria, history, background, etc. and to express themselves in their own words.

4. If you learned something new in the conversation, exchange, or growing friendship, remember to **express gratitude** for

the developing relationship of trust and friendship, and for the joy of that discovery.

In students' words
The value of small group discussions

For me the most impactful moments of the class were the handful of small-group sessions scattered throughout the semester. It was during these classes that we were given the opportunity to interact with our classmates in a way not possible in larger environment. While we were always encouraged and able to share our thoughts in every class, the size of the group and the time constraints of a two-hour class often made true dialog and meaningful exploration of a topic difficult. Breaking out into small groups of only two or three others, however, allowed for a much more probing and nuanced discussion.

One day, in particular, stands out in my mind as an especially thought provoking and meaningful experience. The topic for the class was professional conscience clauses and we were examining an ethics opinion about a lawyer asking to be dismissed from representing a minor seeking an abortion. I had just written a reflection paper in which I had ardently argued that a lawyer's professional obligations should take second place to that lawyer's moral belief system. I was concerned about the dangerous precedent the ethics opinion might have set by requiring lawyers to sacrifice their moral convictions to their professional responsibility.

In my small group I encountered classmates with opposing perspectives. The ensuing discussion—which allowed for probing follow-up questions and constructive feedback on my arguments—helped me to reconsider my hard-line stance and to appreciate the nuance and difficulty in the problem.

Thankfully, my classmates didn't react from either a defensive or offensive posture and I could tell that their goal was not to try to challenge my position. Instead, they responded with kindness and interest in how I came to my conclusions. In this context I felt like I had the space to engage in discussion and meaningfully examine my views. By the end of the class, I had come to appreciate the stances of my classmates and reconsidered my position. This unique environment that had been created turned out to be quite constructive and I think each of us came away from our conversation with a new appreciation for each other's perspectives.

It was in moments like this that I fully embraced the notion that we indeed have a lot to learn from each other if we simply can be present enough to recognize their wisdom and appreciate their perspective. It takes some intentionality to find that stillness in which we are not distracted by outside influences but it is absolutely worth it and it leads to unexpected insights if you approach the process with sincerity. Frankly, I've never allowed myself to be as open and vulnerable in law school as I was with those in my small groups. I found simply having a forum in which I could wrestle with many of my biggest questions about my religion and the law with other smart and caring classmates to be an invaluable experience and a highlight of my time in law school.

Alex S.

Step 5

Learn to Lean into Disagreement and Conflict

THERE IS A RISK THAT FOSTERING such openness in a classroom can open up a Pandora's Box of sensitivities that students and professors alike fear they may violate—perhaps leading even to serious conflict. As discussed more fully in the note below, personal feedback from professors can show students how to step back from strongly held positions in order to empathize with different perspectives and to re-evaluate their claims. Weekly individualized feedback is time-consuming, but it is worth the effort and investment because it allows deep levels of trust to emerge.

Generally, in discussions with highly pluralistic groups, we use a *comparative methodology*. According respect for different systems of thought, each with its own history and claims, allows us to focus our efforts on *understanding* the claims.[8] As an exercise we call attention to how differing definitions of words result in what W.B. Gallie described as "essentially contested concepts."[9] This helps students appreciate the different worldviews and values systems that seminar participants may be operating from. For example, when key words or phrases such as "Progressive" or "Christian Right," or even the concept of "harm" emerge during a discussion, we try to generate a conversation that opens out the layers of meaning so that students can appreciate the different—even clashing—interpretations.

Similarly, we invite students to examine the assumptions that ground the meaning of collective terms such as "we," "us," "they" and "them," to challenge reductive presumptions about shared meaning or shared goals. As team teachers, we also look for opportunities to model disagreement, our different emphases, and our different disciplinary instincts, when those emerge organically in our class discussions.

We scrutinize perspectives all along the spectrum of political stances, as well as varying religious approaches to texts and authority. We want students to understand that our purpose is not to de-stabilize particular belief systems or convictions, but to invite intellectually curious questions about each student's own stance to become aware of how *others* may perceive or process their arguments for a deeply held position or conviction.

At times, we use non-threatening communication tools to show students how to make their perspectives more transparent to each other. In the Appendix we describe tools for fostering greater empathy amid potential conflict.

In students' words
The value of leaning into disagreement

During the semester, a strong disagreement between two students emerged on the issue of abortion. During office hours, both students had asked to be challenged in improving their communication skills, and putting these students in the same group, which at this point in the semester included the exercise of reading each other's papers, offered that possibility.

Ricardo A.: One time during a small group discussion, a classmate who I had otherwise experienced as a very kind person expressed a view on abortion that very much clashed with my own. I felt angry and wanted to explode with arguments to the contrary. Instead, with much frustration, I thought to myself that such a discussion would be useless. I feared I'd be seen as intolerant, and I thought that further talk would probably not resolve our disagreement, so I left it at that.

Jessica G.: While I realized that his opinion was different from my own, I hadn't given due weight to the emotional intensity and depth of a controversial subject such as this one. Instead, I approached the discussion on an entirely academic level. In doing so, however, I realize that I made an assumption about my view being the most "correct," and therefore assumed it would be ubiquitously shared. The moment that Ricardo began to express views quite opposite of mine, I could feel myself shut down. I no longer viewed the conversation as a strictly academic endeavor; it suddenly felt personal.

Ricardo A.: The incident stuck in my head, and a few days later I turned in a reflection about what happened, in which I talked about the difficulty of even talking about these subjects, let alone openly sharing our most closely held beliefs about them. My reflection featured many of the stern replies I would have hurled at my unsuspecting classmate, had I decided to argue. I knew that our reflections for this class would be shared with others for a small group discussion, but I had not envisioned further conversation with this classmate! The cat was out of the bag.

Jessica G.: I too was taken aback because I did not realize how emotional the conversation had felt for both of us, and I was embarrassed that the experience had frustrated Ricardo so deeply.

Ricardo A.: So, after our mutual feelings of embarrassment subsided, my classmate and I embraced the opportunity to have a respectful and productive discussion, regardless of whether it would change anyone's mind. As we shared our views with our hearts set on listening rather than wanting to convince, we cleared enough interpersonal space to allow ourselves to acknowledge the nuances and depth of each other's perspectives, and even the challenges that they posed to our own. As I truly listened to this real person express what she believed and why, her candid explanation slowly replaced the unfair caricature of the other side's view that I now realized I had held in my head. It was heartening to see the same thing happening in the other direction, as my classmate acknowledged that some aspects of my view resonated with her, too. Where there was anger and frustration, now there was kinship and mutual recognition. We had built a bridge, and that strikes me as a very valuable thing.

Jessica G.: There's so much power in seeking to have a conversation to understand another's perspective, and not to change his or her mind. We both have strong, passionate views on an issue such as this one, and we're unlikely to alter the other's stance on a belief so profoundly held. But, we can even learn more about our own perspectives by listening with a true intention of understanding. Some people would say that there's no point in having these types of conversations because you're not going to change someone else's mind. Our experience made me realize that we don't need to change another's mind in order to feel like the conversation was a success. Our own willingness to be open can encourage openness from others. And in that space, there is tremendous opportunity for growth, learning, and understanding.

Accompaniment

The inter-play of private and public space

When possible, consistent and private personal feedback on student submissions can reinforce the communication and community-building skills at the heart of each of the steps. For example, to reinforce the first step, feedback can help students to identify how their habits of mind may be interfering with a more reflective stance and perspective. In a polarized cultural climate, students struggle to overcome what we describe as reflections of their reptilian "fight or flight" reactions. Students in "fight" mode tend to overemphasize the binary debate between two polarities, and thus turn the other side's argument into a straw person that can be easily and dramatically destroyed. Students in "flight" mode pack their oral air time or written word count with non-committal summaries of other people's arguments and observations, avoiding the commitment of taking a defined position. Personal feedback helps them to see how their reductive or binary views prevent them from perceiving the complexity in opposing positions and encourages them to risk articulating their personal stance.

To hone the professional skills that we want them to develop, we often query a student's choice of words and encourage them to examine how others might receive their choices. We also invite them into empathetic thought experiments, to imagine how the principles that they are articulating might be applied in other circumstances. Because this critical work takes place in private space, for example, via email, there is no risk of shaming students in a public setting. Further, our own misunderstandings or misinterpretations as professors can be addressed and corrected in private.

We realize that many of the questions we are examining in class may bring out intense personal pain. Personalized feedback on written submissions can convey our continuous effort to pay close attention not only to what the students say, but also to how their submissions and oral contributions reflect their integrity as human beings. On several occasions, accompanying students personally through some of the questions that came to the surface in their reflection papers has helped in the process of healing inner wounds and finding their voice in the seminar. Often their response to such accompaniment is to "pay it forward" by being especially attentive to the perspectives and sensitivities of their seminar colleagues.

Accompaniment also helps students to apply the communication tools they have developed in class to other areas of their lives. At a certain point in our team-teaching journey, we gleaned from the reflections that spouses, partners, and close friends were curious about the seminar's methods and themes. Some asked to sit in on a class session, but we felt that visitors would disrupt the sense of privacy and trust that we sought. Nonetheless, we wanted to encourage the wider impact the course seemed to be having, and to reflect on how the methods we were using could heal polarization in family, community, and work settings. Late in the semester we hosted a dinner to which students could invite a core "conversation partner" on these difficult questions, and we designed the after-dinner conversation so that these partners could experience how the class worked and what we hoped to convey. The evening invited further reflection on how to "scale out" our experience of healing polarization to other areas of our private, professional, and civic life.

Questions of scale:
Larger settings, fewer resources

The methods described in this book were developed in the context of relatively small seminars (fifteen to eighteen students) in which the goals and expectations were based on personal reflection about values and identity. We chose to focus especially on religious and political differences, but we imagine that the approach would work just as well if applied to other aspects of personal and professional identity. The method would need to be modified for classes that are larger and/or more focused on content-based retention. We also realize that in many areas of college, university, graduate and professional education, reflection papers may not be the optimal teaching method, and that the labor required may not be feasible, especially in very large classes.

Team teaching with someone who embodies significant disciplinary, gender, religious, political, or intellectual difference is a powerful vehicle for breaking through some aspects of polarization. But we also realize that in some circumstances, financial and time constraints may not permit this option.

In settings that differ from ours, it is possible to choose one or two areas where significant differences in perspective are likely, and prepare an agenda for class discussion based on reflection papers or short blurbs submitted prior to that particular class. Even in large classes, breaking into small groups or pairs may help students come into vital contact with people who hold different perspectives. It would be also interesting to survey how the use of tools for immediate anonymous feedback to general questions (such as clickers) has produced similar results to using an agenda based on reflection papers. The basic strategy, we think, is to allow students to see that they are not alone in their opinions.

Finally, even in a very large group, an exercise in pairs such as one outlined in the Appendix may help students practice "listening to understand," and thus experience how conversation across profound difference is not only possible but enriching.

Appendix

Exercise: "Listening to Understand"[10]

Introductive Talking Points: The goal of this exercise is not to win an argument, nor to sort out whether you agree or disagree. Instead, the goal is to hone the skill of listening to understand.

Some suggestions:

1. Unplug from technology and cell phones; consider how your body language can convey openness and attention.

2. Be open to how the other person is expressing their position in their own categories and words. As you repeat back what the other person said, if you encounter something that you don't fully understand, ask sincere questions that leave the other space to frame the new information according to their own criteria, history, background, etc.

3. If you learned something new in the conversation, exchange or growing friendship, express gratitude and convey to the other the joy of that discovery.

Pair off and pick a topic (suggestions below, feel free to identify a topic not on the list) on which you anticipate some disagreement.

1. First person shares their perspective on the topic for 2 minutes (3 minutes max).

2. Second person shares what they understood about the first person's perspective for 2 minutes.

3. First person has an opportunity to correct or refine their impression of what the second person may have not completely understood or appreciated (2 minutes).

4. Switch roles, with the second person going first, to share their perspective; repeat the process.

5. Take 2-3 minutes to reflect (individually or together) on insights regarding the listening process; feel free to share these insights when we come back together as a large group.

[Follow with a plenary session to share insights that the exercise generated.]

Areas of Potential Political Disagreement

[List relevant topics, depending on context]

Exercise: "What is at Stake for You?"

During a discussion about a difficult topic, one may feel overwhelmed by a need to express one's own perspective, and thus it becomes a struggle to be attentive to another person's concerns. Let's start this conversation with fresh awareness of what may be at stake for another person in the conversation.

1. Sit next to a person with whom you have not been grouped before.

2. Ask your colleague: what is at stake for you in our conversation today? If helpful, jot down a few key words or ideas on an index card.

3. Be attentive to your partner's questions / concerns throughout our discussions today.

4. When _both_ of your concerns have been discussed to your satisfaction as a team, raise the index card as a signal to our seminar. At the break we will tally the voices we have not yet heard, and the mini-agendas not yet covered.

5. Toward the end of class, we will leave a moment to reflect on the difference made by this deliberate attention to at least one other person's concerns.

Variant prior to broaching an especially sensitive subject:
Ask your colleague: what most concerns you or worries you about broaching this topic as we enter this discussion today? Be attentive to these concerns throughout the discussion.

Communication Tool: The SOS Card

This tool emerged in the context of a conflict between a student from the religious majority in the seminar who had inadvertently hurt one student from a religious minority. Few of the students were sensitive enough to pick up on the nuance. Reflecting on this particular conflict led to developing a tool to raise awareness of unintentional harm, and to foster learning for the future. "SOS" can stand for either "Step into the Other Side" or "Save Our Seminar." The card itself was simply an index card with "SOS" printed on one side. It was introduced at a point in the class dynamic when there was enough trust to propose using it following these ground rules:

- You may raise the SOS card whether your concern emerges from your own personal identity or from an empathetic concern about what others might be feeling.

- Concerns may cover a range of questions and concerns, including political stance or identity (race, ethnicity, class, religion, gender, sexual orientation, etc.).

- As a class, we agree to receive the SOS signal not as an accusation or a threat, but as a suggestion to bring additional layers of complexity and empathy into our conversations.

- We agree to give priority to these flags in the timing of our conversation, so as to profit in real time from these suggestions for further attentiveness.

Notes

1. Pew Research Center, *The Partisan Divide on Political Values Grows Even Wider* (October 5, 2017) http://www.people-press.org/2017/10/05/the-partisan-divide-on-political-values-grows-even-wider/.

2. Hayley Glatter, *The Most Polarized Freshman Class in Half a Century*, The Atlantic (May 2, 2017).

3. Pew Research Center, *Millennials: A Portrait of Generation Next* at page 2 (Feb. 2010), http://pewresearch.org/millennials/. *See generally* MORLEY WINOGRAD & MICHAEL D. HAIS, MILLENNIAL MOMENTUM: HOW A NEW GENERATION IS REMAKING AMERICA (2011).

4. This book also includes examples from Amy Uelmen's seminar in *Religion & the Work of the Lawyer*.

5. On occasion we have discerned the need to leave more leeway for the students to decide when to enter into the conversation, and so we circulate topics but not names. Similarly, when essays are characterized by deep personal pain or anger, we have reached out to students individually to help them discern what elements of their reflection (if any) they wish to make public.

6. Cindi May, *Students are Better Off without a Laptop in the Classroom*, Scientific American (July 11, 2017).

7. *See* e.g., Simon Sinek interview with Tom Bilyeu, "Millennials in the Workplace," *Inside Quest* https://www.youtube.com/watch?v=5MC2X-LRbkE, at minute 11.57, describing how cell phone habits impede the formation of relationships in the workplace.

8. Legal scholar Robert Cover is an inspiration for our work in this area. *See, e.g.*, Robert Cover, *Obligation: A Jewish Jurisprudence of the Social Order*, Journal of Law & Religion 5 (1987-1988): 65. *See also* Amelia J. Uelmen, *Mapping a Method for Dialogue: Exploring the Tension between Razian Autonomy and Catholic Solidarity as Applied to Euthanasia* J. Moral Theology v.2, n.2 (2013) 133-155 (discussing Cover).

9. W.B. Gallie, *Essentially Contested Concepts*, Procedures of the Aristotelian Society 56 (1955-56): 167-98.

10. Many thanks to Jim Funk, JL Funk & Associates, for the initial ideas for this exercise developed for a series of community-based workshops on healing polarization.

New City Press

Hyde Park, New York

New City Press is one of more than 20 publishing houses sponsored by the Focolare, a movement founded by Chiara Lubich to help bring about the realization of Jesus' prayer: "That all may be one" (John 17:21). In view of that goal, New City Press publishes books and resources that enrich the lives of people and help all to strive toward the unity of the entire human family. We are a member of the Association of Catholic Publishers.

Other Books in the *5* Step Series

www.newcitypress.com

Scan to join our mailing list for discounts and promotions

Periodicals
Living City Magazine

www.livingcitymagazine.com